A JOURNEY TO WHOLENESS

VICKTORY EICHELBERGER

ISBN-13: 978-0-9997607-3-4
ISBN-10: 0-9997607-3-4

Table of Contents

INTRODUCTION
PACKING FOR THE JOURNEY

As you start this journey with your hand in God's hand, He will lead your heart and soul to completeness and wholeness in Him. We pray that you will allow God to fill the void that may be present in your life today. He knows exactly where you are mentally, emotionally, physically, and spiritually; where you have been; what challenges you are facing or have faced; and how to best bring about the necessary change that will get you unstuck and moving. There are things you will want to move forward with, but there are some things you will need to leave behind.

It is important to discern where you are in order to know what direction you are going. This journey may be challenging because of the pain associated with it. Ask God to navigate you through this journey of unfamiliar territory. Look to the hill where your help comes from. By looking to the LORD, you put yourself under His protection and commit yourself to His care.

As you begin this journey, you must:

- **Prepare your heart to receive:** *"Search me, O God, and know my heart' test my thoughts. Point out anything you find in me that makes you sad, and lead me along the path of everlasting life" (Psalm 139-23-24).*

Prepare your heart to receive, Ask the Holy Spirit to reveal anything that is not pleasing to Him.

Prepare means establish, fix, and prepare to apply. Posture yourself to receive from God. Put away any negative thoughts that would keep you from hearing from God. A forgiven heart is a must on this journey. It would be impossible to move forward productively if you chose not to forgive. Ask God to remove anything that would hinder you from making progress or moving forward on this journey.

- **Commit to Prayer:** *"Pray at all times. Whatever things that may happen to you, continue to thank God. God wants you to do this because you are united to Christ Jesus" (1 Thessalonians 5:17-18).*

Do not start your journey without asking for God's guidance. This is very important on this journey. Prayer is an intimate relationship between you and God. It will be difficult to hear and comprehend what God is communicating to you if you do not know His voice. John 10:27 tells us, *"My sheep know hear my voice, and I know them, and they follow me. I will give them eternal life, and they will never perish, and no one will snatch them out of my hand."*

- **Check Your Attitude and Your Mindset:** *"For as he thinks in his heart, so is he [in behavior-one who manipulates]. He says to you, "Eat and drink, "Yet his heart is not with you (but it is begrudging the cost)" (Proverbs 23:7).*

If your thoughts are negative, we only expect negative results. But if your thoughts are positive, then we expect positive results. Your mindset is the foundation for the results you will experience in your life. It is a collection of your feelings, emotions, behaviors, and beliefs.

Be open to hearing what God is revealing to you through the Holy Spirit. Do not be so quick to dismiss those things He reveals to you that you do not necessarily agree with. These could be blind spots. Blind spots are negative behaviors that we possess but are not willing to acknowledge, but everyone around us can see them. Carl Jung called them our "shadow." A "shadow" is a repressed side of a human being's personality. In order to heal, your thoughts must be positive.

- **Allow Yourself to be Vulnerable to the leading of God's Spirit:** *"Behold, I stand at the door, and knock. If any man hears my voice and opens the door, I will come in to him, and will sup with him, and he with me" (Revelation 3:20).*

Being vulnerable is simply saying, "God, I trust you!" It is painful to think about our shortcomings, mistakes, flaws, and wounds. This is precisely why we need God. What good is it to ask for God's love if we are not willing to allow that love to penetrate to the depths of our hearts, where we really need it? By allowing oneself to be stripped of their ego and opening up their hearts, one can better understand and appreciate the covenant and love of God. When you completely surrender to your rights and to God's rights, you will begin to see healing manifest in your life. When God is present within you, He will protect you. Psalm 121:5-6 tells us, *"The LORD will guard you; He is by your side to protect you. The sun will not hurt you during the day, nor the moon during the night. The LORD will protect you from all danger; He will keep you sage. He will protect you as you come and go, now and forever."*

- **Be Alert:** *Pay careful attention to your own work, for then you will bet the satisfaction of a job well done, and you won't need to compare yourself to anyone else. For each responsible for our own conduct"* (Galatians 6:4-5).

One of the hardest things for some people to do is not compare themselves to others. Understand that this is your journey. Comparing your journey to others can be a stumbling block to what God is trying to do in you. Although you and others may have traveled the same road, your experience may have been different; therefore, your healing will be different.

- **Set Boundaries in Advance:** *"Being clear about your no and your yes is a theme of the Bible. Let your yes be yes and your no be no"* (Matthew 5:7).

The Positive Woman by Gael Lindenfield talks about the boundaries we should set. "The purpose of having boundaries is to protect and take care of ourselves. We need to be able to tell other people when they are acting in ways that are not acceptable to us. The first step is to realize we have a right to protect and defend ourselves; that not only do we have the right, but it is our duty to take responsibility for how we allow others to treat us." It is important to set boundaries with individuals who will hinder you from reaching your healthy place.

- **Study and Apply the Word on this Journey:** *"Your words are what sustain me; they are food to my hungry soul. They bring joy to my sorrowing heart and delight me"* (Jeremiah 15:16).

The Word of God is substance and nurture for our soul. It will strengthen us in times of need. When we do not understand the journey, we will trust the process of what God is doing. For God's grace is sufficient for you; for when you are weak, you are strengthened by His power. Proverbs 4:20-22 tells us that "God's word is a lamp to our feet and a light to our path." Psalm 119:105 tells us, "The Word will lead you and give you guidance when you are not sure."

Each person's journey will be different. However, healing will not happen until you begin. This journey will result in a more fulfilled, loving, and abundant life, as well as a renewed sense of hope and purpose. You will have a closer relationship with God, which will allow you to see yourself as God sees you and walk in your intended purpose.

No one can travel this journey for you. You must be an active participant to get where God wants to take you.

At the end of each chapter, you will find a reflection page. This page will give you the opportunity to journal your thoughts about the emotions that you felt. The purpose is to uncover the hurt and deepen your understanding of what took place so you can heal. Also, at the end of the book, you will find a place to journal.

You have **EVERYTHING** To become who **GOD CREATED** You to be!

CHAPTER ONE

THE WHOLE ME:
GOD'S PURPOSE AND PLAN

"For I know the plans I have for you," declares the LORD, "plans to prosper you
and not to harm you, plans to give you hope and a future."
JEREMIAH 29:11

It was never God's intent for mankind to suffer or fail. In the beginning, man was created whole. They were created in the image and likeness of The Father, The Son, and the Holy Ghost (Genesis 1:26-27). Everything God created was perfectly created. God created the universe and everything in six days, and at the end of His creation, He looked at everything He had made and declared it to be very good (Genesis 1:31). His original creation was beautiful and full of joy, and He had placed mankind in a perfect paradise with everything provided for them. In Genesis 1:29–30, the Lord said, "See, I have given you every herb that yields seed that is on the face of all the earth and every tree whose fruit yields seed; to you it shall be for food." "Also, to every beast of the earth, to every bird of the air, and to everything that creeps on the earth, in which there is life, I have given every green herb for food." However, then sin happened.

Satan came to Eve in the Garden and tempted her to eat from the tree that God had commanded Adam not to eat from—the tree of the knowledge of good and evil. After disobeying God's command, both Adam and Eve's eyes were opened, and they became aware of good and evil, right and wrong. Because of this disobedience, Adam fell from a perfectly-created, whole soul to a ruined soul. At this time, mankind lost fellowship with God as it once was, and sin entered the world. As descendants of Adam, we now enter a world separated from God. Because of sin, we also ceased to understand God's characters, plans, and purposes. However, God has a plan to restore us to His original plan through the sacrifice of His only begotten son.

Seeing Things From God's View

Many of us wrestle with who God has created us to be. This can be due to our not having the ability to see ourselves as God sees us. If I don't see myself as worthy of what I desire to be, then I will not put forth the effort to become who God created me to be.

To see ourselves as God sees us, we must first understand who God says we are. Seeing things from God's perspective is crucial in order to know what His plan is for you. Perspective is defined as understanding, wisdom, and discernment. In other words, you must be able to see the bigger picture than what your natural eyes are able to see and what your human mind can comprehend.

I remember when God revealed to me who I was created to be for Him. I questioned whether He knew what and who He was choosing. I questioned it because I did not see myself as God saw me. I did not think of myself the way God thought of me. For so long, I had negative words spoken over me that all I imagined myself to be were those words. I saw myself as broken and unusable. He saw me as valuable and effective for the kingdom. With the help of the Holy Spirit, I was able to see myself as God sees me. However, God saw me differently. Isaiah 55:8-9: The LORD said, "For My thoughts are not your thoughts, and My ways are not your ways," says the Lord. "Because the heavens are higher than the earth, so are My ways higher than your ways, and My thoughts higher than your thoughts."

So many of us find ourselves basing our sense of self-worth on what someone has said about us, how others see us, or the mistakes we have made. None of this has any bearing on how God sees and feels about us. He said, "He knows the plan He has for our lives." Do you not know that God is all-knowing, and when He developed the plan, He knew the mistakes you would make, the pain you would endure, and the people who would not like you and turn their backs on you? Yet He still deemed you worthy. As a result, take comfort in who God has chosen you to be. Jesus tells us in John 15:16, "It was not you who chose me, but I (the LORD), who chose you and appointed you to go and bear fruit that would remain, so that whatever you ask the Father in my name, He may give you." He also reminds us in John 15:18, "If the people of this world hate you, just remember that they hated Me (Jesus) first." Therefore, take pleasure in what God is doing in your life.

Who Does God Say I Am?

I am a branch of the true vine and a conduit of Christ's life.	**John 15: 5**
I am a friend of Jesus.	**John 15:12-17**
I have been justified freely by His grace through the redemption that came by Christ Jesus.	**Romans 3:24**
I will not be condemned by God; I have been set free from the law of sin and death.	**Romans 8:2**
As a child of God, I am a fellow heir with Christ.	**Romans 8:17**
In Christ Jesus, I have wisdom, righteousness, sanctification, and redemption.	**1 Corinthians 1:30**
I am a new creature in Christ.	**2 Corinthians 5:17**
I have become the righteousness of God in Christ.	**2 Corinthians 5:21**
I have an inheritance.	**Ephesians 1:9-11**
I have been sealed with the Holy Spirit of promise.	**Ephesians 1:13**
Because of God's mercy and love, I have been made alive with Christ.	**Ephesians 2:4-5**
I am seated in heavenly places with Christ.	**Ephesians 2:6**
I am God's workmanship created to produce good works.	**Ephesians 2:10**
I have been brought near to God by the blood of Christ.	**Ephesians 2:13**
I am a member of Christ's body and a partaker of His promise.	**Ephesians 3:6; Ephesians 5:30**
I have boldness and confident access to God through faith in Christ.	**Ephesians 3:12**
I am righteous and holy.	**Ephesians 4:22-24**
I am light in the Lord.	**Ephesians 5:8**
I am a citizen of heaven.	**Philippians 3:20**

I have been made complete in Christ.	**Colossians 2:9-10**
I have been raised with Christ.	**Colossians 3:1**
I have been chosen by God. I am holy and beloved.	**Colossians 3:12**
My life is hidden with Christ in God.	**Colossians 3:3**
God loves me and has chosen me.	**Colossians 3:12-14**
I have been made one with all who are in Christ Jesus.	**Galatians 3:28**
I am no longer a slave but a child of an heir.	**Galatians 4:7**
I have been blessed with every spiritual blessing in the heavenly places.	**Ephesians 1:3**
I am CHOSEN, holy, and blameless before God.	**Ephesians 1:4**

1. What I learned about me from God's perspective?

2. What makes me special?

3. I am worthy of...

I AM...

Write a letter of love to yourself in which you make affirmations like, "I am worthy, and I deeply adore myself for who I am."

This kind of letter is intended to increase your sense of self-worth and self-compassion as well as your appreciation for the deeds you have accomplished and the life you have led. People who have trouble being friendly to themselves will do well to write themselves this kind of letter. It enables you to consider how you might improve your individual self-care and self-assurance.

_____

_____

_____

_____

_____

_____

_____

_____

_____

_____

_____

_____

_____

_____

_____

_____

_____

_____

_____

_____

_____

_____

_____

_____

_____

_____

_____

REFLECTIONS

PRAYERS

CHAPTER TWO

THE WHOLE JOURNEY:
BECOMING ME

"For we are workmanship created in Christ Jesus for good works, which
God prepared beforehand that we should walk in them.
EPHESIANS 2:10

First and foremost, God desires that each of us be whole.This is who He created us to be. "Whole" is defined as the state of being perfectly well in body, soul (mind, will, and emotions), and spirit—complete sanctification and restoration. Strong's Dictionary describes the Greek word for whole as *holos.* combining form meaning "whole" or "entire." The wholeness God has for us happens from the inside out. It begins with the heart. To get to a whole place, you must first understand what it means to be whole in God so that you can identify what wholeness is not.Wholeness does not mean perfection.

Not only is it essential to know who God says we are, but it is also crucial to know who God is! You may be asking yourself lots of questions in relation to wholeness: What is wholeness? What does it mean to feel or be whole? How do you become whole? How do you see yourself as whole, especially when all you have ever felt is hurt?

It is trusting God to do everything that He has promised in His word, with the understanding that on this journey called life, we will encounter some hardships, heartaches, and disappointments, but that doesn't mean God has forfeited the promise He has made concerning us; we will not become discouraged and quit when we are faced with life's challenges. Every trial, test, and tribulation we face will make us stronger.

1. Suffering produces intimacy with our Father (Job 42:5)
2. Suffering produces growth and maturity (James 1:2-4)
3. Suffering conforms us into our Father's original intents (Romans 8:28-30).

Acknowledging what happened to me was key to my healing, and I must say, it was one of the hardest things I've ever had to do. I was forced to deal with the emotions of hurt, pain, and betrayal. I had to come face-to-face with myself and how anger consumed me. I had to choose healing or being bound by pain. My choice was to heal. For far too long, I had allowed my condition to keep me from receiving God's blessings. It was time to heal.

It is important to deal with the issues of your past. If you do not, it will continue to control you in the present and shape your future.

Our past experiences, whether positive or negative, are a series of lessons that help shape who we have become to this very point. How we think about or view our past will determine the outcome of our becoming. You will uncover and reveal self-esteem and self-worth issues that each of you may be facing that can prevent you from knowing who you are as an individual, valuing your worth, and reaching your full potential. We will identify internal prohibiting factors such as lingering hurt, which can damage, cripple, and even paralyze your future. An important part of your recovery is discovery. You will need to identify internal impediments, such as lingering pain, that can prevent you from moving forward.

Many times, our childhood experiences are so damaging that they prevent us from moving forward. Beginning this process will bring back some memories you may choose not to deal with, but it is necessary. In order to heal from the past, you will need to acknowledge the present. Your present anger! your present bitterness! Your present hurts! Your present brokenness There are things that happened in your past but are still living in your future! Oftentimes, we try to cover it up, but it is obvious. We wear masks and think we are good to go, but we really are not.

Many of us spend our lives wearing masks to conceal aspects of ourselves that we don't want others to see or know about us, things that might change how they perceive us as individuals.The problem with wearing these masks is that we don't allow people to see our true selves. But not only that, we forget who our true selves are because we have learned to wear a mask.

For the longest time, I did not know who I was. I had lost my true self at an early age when I was sexually abused. As a result, I struggled in my presence.What I came to find out was that a scared little girl was living within me, needing to be healed so that the healthy woman I needed to be could come forward. Therefore, I had to take care of the little girl. I knew in order for her to heal, I would need to address her every concern, worry, hurt, and disappointment. I had to assure her it was okay for her to emerge as this woman who desperately needed to come forth. I had to unmask my pain so I could walk into my destiny. I had carried around a façade for so long, but it was time for me to face my issues head-on. No more excuses! I had to stop allowing anger to rule me, so I had to go to the broken little girl.

She was about seven years old. She had built this wall around her for protection and had her guard up. She was deeply broken and angry. She had lost her way and did not know who she was. For some reason, she trusted me.

and allowed me in. I felt the hurt, the pain, the brokenness, and the betrayal. She was ashamed and embarrassed about the inappropriate things that had happened to her. Getting in touch with our inner child can be scary because we will have to unearth things we may not be ready to face, but it is necessary to heal the inner child. I began to have a dialogue with her.

Making a connection with my inner hurt was necessary for my inner healing. Understand that the greatest change will come when you can connect to your inner self, see your suffering, and make a conscious decision to make a change. Acknowledging I was broken was the first step in my journey of healing. If I did not acknowledge it, I would not position myself to make the necessary change. As I began my journey, it did not feel good. I was exposed! There was a grieving process I had to go through. The little girl in me was not only broken, but she was angry. And I had to deal with it. No one else could change the way I felt. This was all on me.

Most times, when we are in a broken place, we do not want to admit our brokenness and that we need healing. So often, we walk around as if we have everything together and think that because we have not told anyone, they cannot see it. However, it is impossible to miss a cistern that is cracked. This was me. I had to take responsibility for my healing, or my actions would keep repeating themselves. I had to learn "me," but not only who I was, but also how to love myself.

You must learn to accept every part of you—every quirk, every flaw, every part of you!

Accepting who you are is crucial on this journey. It is critical to embrace the true you, not who others want you to be, not the person you have pretended to be, but the person you are sometimes afraid to let people see because it is different, which is not necessarily a bad thing, but it may make you stand out like a sore thumb.

When you unmask the real problem, the underlying root of the issues, you will be able to accept yourself for who God says you are. Discovering my true identity was key to me becoming the woman God was calling forth.

You must be patient with your healing process. It will take time; therefore, do not become frustrated. It may or may not happen as quickly as you would like. There are things that you will heal from instantly, and then there are some things that He will take His time to heal. He knows you better than anyone else, so accept His process.

The enemy has been plotting against you your entire life, even before you were born. His desire is to keep you from being in a healthy place and becoming the person God has called you to be. Once you unmask the enemy, you will be able to heal.

MY STORY

My Past Self: Write a letter from your present self to your past self, encouraging healing. Address any significant issues you had in your life at that point in time, offer your past self love and forgiveness, and be compassionate and empathetic, reassuring your past self with love and kindness. Exploring the issues fully while being empathetic towards yourself will give you the closure you need for that period in your life.

This type of letter can help you dig deeper into underlying challenges you may have so you may heal, gain clarity, and get some closure.

Spend some time praying and asking God to perform a supernatural work in your heart that will allow you to forgive the person who has caused you pain.

_____

_____

_____

_____

_____

_____

_____

_____

_____

_____

_____

_____

_____

_____

_____

_____

_____

_____

_____

_____

_____

_____

_____

_____

_____

MY STORY

My Future Self: Write a letter from your present self to your future self. Write as if you are communicating with a close friend. Identify where you are in life (physically, emotionally, mentally, and spiritually), the things you are going through, and any dreams, hopes, visions, goals, healing, etc., you desire for your future self. What will you do differently now that would get you there?

_____

_____

_____

_____

_____

_____

_____

_____

_____

_____

_____

_____

_____

_____

_____

_____

_____

_____

_____

_____

_____

_____

_____

_____

_____

_____

_____

_____

PAIN DOESN'T HAVE TO
BE A DEAD END,
IT CAN BE A ROAD THAT
LEADS YOU TO
Your Purpose!

1. What role do anger, bitterness, and unforgiveness play in your life?

2. How much energy do you think you spend daily managing these negative emotions?

3. What do you need to do to change these emotions?

<u>REFLECTIONS</u>

<u>PRAYER</u>

CHAPTER THREE

THE WHOLE HEART:
LETTING GO AND LETTING GOD

"The heart is hopelessly dark and deceitful, a puzzle that no one can figure out. But I, God, search the heart and examine the mind. I get to the heart of the human. I get to the root of things. I treat Them as they really, not as they pretend to be."
JEREMIAH 17:9-10; MSG

Have you ever held a grudge so deep that all you could do was think about the person you were holding it against and how you wanted to get revenge? Or have you ever been so angry with a person that you could not think straight? This can be exhausting. But not only is it exhausting, it can affect you emotionally, mentally, and physically. I know because I have been there.

In order for me to heal and move forward, I knew I needed peace of mind and a healed heart. Therefore, I had to forgive those who had caused me pain. There was no way around it. Forgiving them was for me. Trying to move beyond the wounds that were embedded deeply in my heart by pushing them aside was not working. I needed peace for my well-being, health, and ability to function rationally. Many have a misconception of what forgiveness is and what one must do after they have forgiven someone, so I want to talk about what forgiveness is not.

Forgiveness is not forgetting. It does not excuse the person for their actions. It's not pretending it never happened. Forgiveness doesn't mean the hurt will automatically disappear. It doesn't mean you have to trust the person. It is not reconciliation. Forgiveness does not mean I have to have a relationship with the person. It does not mean I condone or excuse the person's behavior. But what forgiveness is is "choosing" to forgive the person for what they did; it is letting go of the anger, bitterness, and hatred that have consumed you. It is liberating yourself to live the abundant life that Christ intended.

Just as we expect God to forgive us, He expects us to forgive others. Matthew 6:14 and Ephesians 4:32 teach us that a person who is not willing to forgive others will find it difficult to receive their healing. Unforgiveness breeds anger, anger breeds bitterness, bitterness breeds hatred, and so on. Forgiveness is something we all want but seldom want to give. Jesus taught about the essence of forgiveness. In Matthew 6:14–15, He said, *"If you forgive those who sin against you, your Heavenly Father will forgive you. But if you refuse to forgive others, your Father will not forgive your sin."*

Letting go may be difficult for you if you feel like you need an apology to move on. When we have been hurt, we yearn for an apology. We need the person to admit their mistake so we can move on. It may never happen. However, we cannot remain in a place of anger, hoping one day the person will apologize. This is a saying by Buddha. *"Holding on to anger is like grasping a hot coal with the intent of throwing it at someone else, only you are the one who gets burned"* or *"Holding a grudge is like drinking poison and waiting for the other person to die."*

Have you ever been so upset about something someone did to you that you became angry and bitter, and that is all you passed on? However, you can't see it because of your blind spots.

It takes a huge amount of energy to remain angry. Accept that the apology may never come, and you are only hurting yourself when you operate in anger. You have to stop seeing yourself as a victim in order to do this. Just because you refuse to forgive an individual does not mean they are not forgiven. Jesus forgives those who seek forgiveness, and He doesn't need your approval.

It may be hard to let go if you have not come to a place where you completely trust God and are able to surrender yourself to Him. Your vulnerability doesn't always mean someone is taking advantage of you. Being weak before God means you can be strengthened "in" Him. 2 Corinthians 12:10 states, "Therefore I take pleasure in infirmities, reproaches, necessities, persecutions, and distress for Christ's sake; for when I am weak, then am I strong."

Recognize the value of forgiveness and how it can improve your life. It sets you up to receive God's blessings and puts you on the path of freedom, peace, and self-empowerment.

Heart Mapping

What does your heart reveal? The heart will disclose its condition. Proverbs 4:23 tells us, "Watch over your heart with all diligence, for from it flow the issues of life."

The focus of this activity is to guide you into awareness of where you are presently and where you would like to be. Take your time and spend serious time on your heart map. Take breaks if needed. Think about the people, places, or things that are most important to you. Start from the center of the heart and work your way outward.

To help you uncover what is in your heart, use the following questions as a guide. Being honest about your pain is very important.

- What are some experiences or central events you will never forget?
- What special moments stand out to you?
- What has really affected your heart?
- What has stayed in your heart?
- What happy or sad memories do you have?
- What secrets have you held in your heart?
- What is important to you?
- What is at the center of your heart?
- What is outside of your heart?

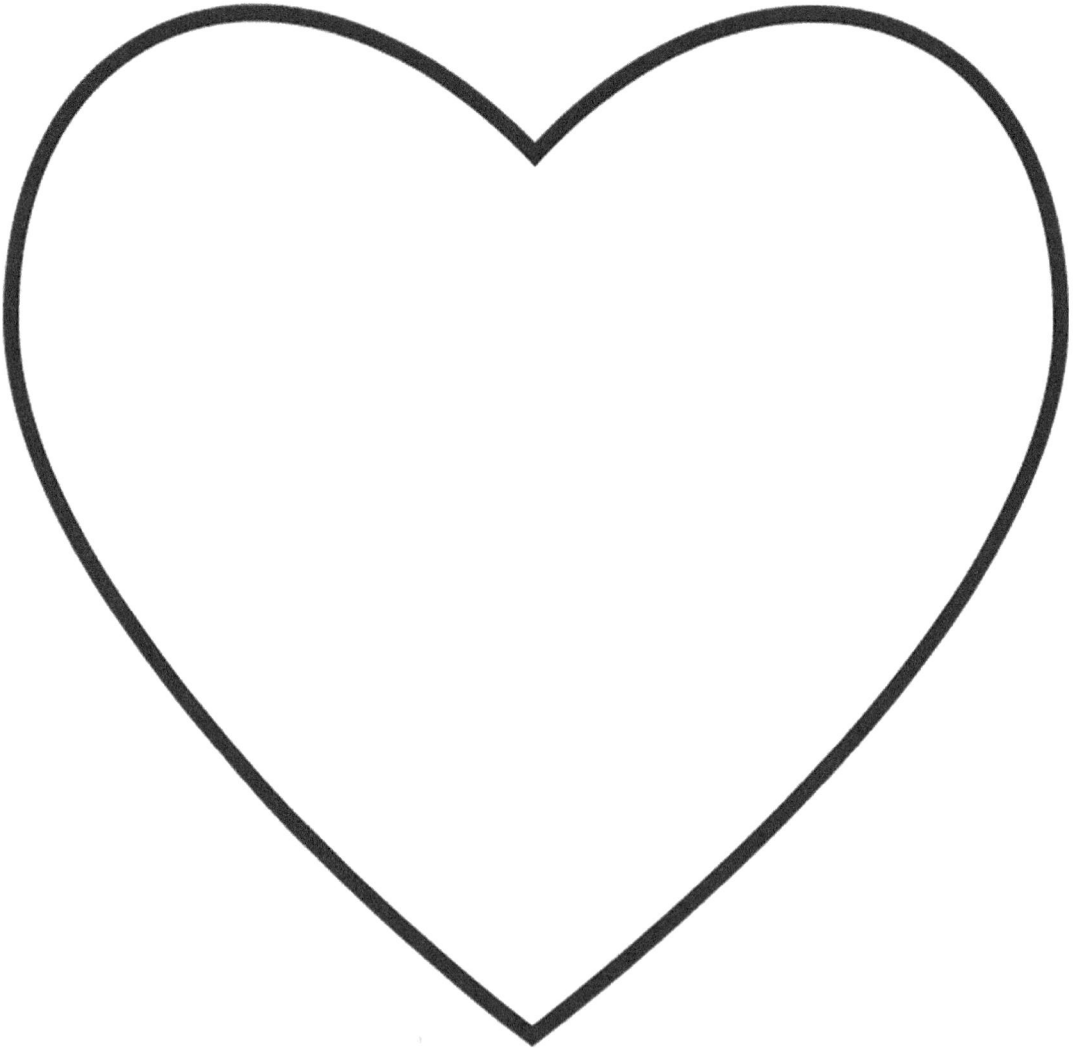

A Heart That
FORGIVES
Is A Heart That
HEALS!

VICKTORY EICHELBERGER

<u>REFLECTIONS</u>

<u>PRAYER</u>

CHAPTER FOUR

THE WHOLE MIND:
REPOSITIONING MY THINKING

"Finally, brothers and sisters, whatever is true, whatever is noble, whatever is right, whatever is pure, whatever is lovely, whatever is admirable-if anything is excellent or praiseworthy- think about such things."
PHILIPPIANS 4:8

Besides a change of heart, one of the most important things you will need to do on this journey is to renew your mind. Renewing your mind means putting off your own negative and corrupt thinking and setting it on the things of Christ.

Your attitude will play a crucial role in how you maneuver through your journey. Awareness of your thoughts is paramount to how you feel. An attitude is a state of mind that is either negative or positive. A negative attitude will hinder you from experiencing your best journey, while a positive attitude will empower you to keep pressing on. Start focusing on the positive aspects of the situations instead of solely on the negative.

1 Peter 1:13 tells us, *"Therefore, prepare our minds for action; keep sober in spirit; fix your hope completely on the grace to be brought to you at the revelation of Jesus Christ."*

Ephesians 4:22-24: *"You were taught with regard to your former way of life to put off your old self, which is being corrupted by its deceitful desires; to be made new in the attitude of your minds; and put on the new self, created to be like God in true righteousness and holiness."*

Not only must you stop thinking in one direction to renew your mind, but you must also think positively. According to Matthew 12:43–45, when an impure spirit leaves a person, it searches for another host before returning to the house it left. However, when it gets there and discovers that the house has not been cleaned, is unorganized, and is without the Spirit of God, it brings in seven other evil spirits and moves in. The situation is worse than it was in the beginning.

When you allow God to change your thinking, your attitude will change. The way you think and speak has the potential to alter your life.

I used to think the worst of myself. I did not think I was worthy of anything good. It was early in my life when my mind became powerless against negative thoughts. My mind became a prey to the enemy because it was exposed and unprotected. Like everything else, it was broken. However, because of my relationship with the Father, I have altered the way I speak to myself. There is good in me. I am aware of this because God looked at everything He created and said, "Not only was it good, but it was very good." However, sin and the outside world had forced me to evaluate who I was in light of my experiences in life. But as I altered my perspective, my environment also changed. made me look at myself based on what I had experienced in life. But when I changed my thoughts, things around me changed. If you want to change the way you feel, change the way you think.

1. In order to change your beliefs, you must understand where your negative thinking comes from. Are you able to identify your negative thinking pattern? What are they?
2. Once you have identified your negative thinking patterns, gather the courage to focus on changing them. What actions or steps do you need to take?
3. Positive Thinking Exercise:
    a. Write down the things you love about you.
    b. Create a gratitude journal.
    c. Speak positive affirmation to yourself.

Write a letter to yourself encouraging you to let go of negative emotions. We frequently suppress our unpleasant feelings as a result of the unfortunate events in our lives. Anger, resentment, bitterness, discord, melancholy, brokenheartedness, and other negative emotions are examples.

The goal of this type of letter is to let everything out so you can move on. Think of forgiving yourself and anyone who has caused you harm.

_____

_____

_____

_____

_____

_____

_____

_____

_____

_____

_____

_____

_____

<u>REFLECTIONS</u>

<u>PRAYERS</u>

CHAPTER FIVE

THE WHOLE TRUTH:
TAKING RESPONSIBILITY

"Commit to the Lord whatever you do, and your plans will succeed."
PROVERBS 16:3

We must accept responsibility for our pain if we are to recover from it. Accepting responsibility means realizing that pain exists and that you are solely responsible for your own recovery.

People will hurt you; that is true, but it is up to you to decide if the wound will prevent you from moving on in a healthy way.

Hurt will inevitably come to us at some point in our lives. Nevertheless, just because we feel upset doesn't imply we have to stay hurt. Although the pain may not have been under your control, your recovery is.

You must be responsible for improving yourself. There might indeed be people there.

Understanding where you are now is essential to understanding where you are heading on a physical, emotional, mental, and spiritual level. It's crucial to be honest with yourself about where you are and what role you played in getting there.

In order to heal, you will need to address the problems that may have prevented you from realizing your worth in God. These things include challenges with self-worth and self-esteem that you may have already experienced or are currently experiencing.

Self-esteem refers to your perception of yourself, your thoughts about yourself, and your opinions of yourself. When you don't feel good about yourself, you'll turn to other people for approval, and when that doesn't happen, you'll start to feel unworthy. You have to learn this.

You must realize that God has already validated you, and that is what matters.

Low self-esteem is greatly influenced by past aches, disappointments, and hurts. Therefore, if you can concentrate on what caused the unpleasant events in your life—whether they were recent or in the past—we may start to improve our self-esteem by getting rid of what initially made us feel this way. The past cannot be changed, but we can learn from it, develop from it, and improve as a result.

Although pain transformed me, I did not let it stop me. You should turn to God when you are in pain. You will be strengthened by God as you seek Him, for when you are weak, you are made strong.

Trauma can develop blind spots in our lives that can become roadblocks and lead to issues with self-esteem. Blind spots are character flaws that you have yet to recognize as actual issues; as a result, you injure both yourself and other people. They are the proverbial elephant in the room.

The parts of ourselves that we are not entirely aware of are referred to as our "blind spots." It could be brought on by our own convictions, principles, routines, emotions, thoughts, etc.

In Isaiah 55:8–9, the LORD said, *"For My thoughts are not your thoughts, and My ways are not your ways," says the Lord. "Because the heavens are higher than the earth, so are My ways higher than your ways, and My thoughts higher than your thoughts."*

Because of this blind spot, we may prevent God from working in and through us because of how we see ourselves, which may differ from how others see us. A blind spot is similar to when your eyesight is obstructed while you are driving an automobile. You have to rapidly look over your shoulder to see what is next to you that you cannot see in your rearview or side mirrors. Before changing lanes, always look over your shoulder to avoid accidents. Neglected spiritual blind spots might keep you stranded or lead to issues in your life.

The Bible does not specifically speak about blind spots; however, blind spots can be a problem. Matthew 7:5 instructs us, *"You hypocrite! "First take the log out of your own eye, and then you will be able to see clearly to take the speck out of your brother's eye."* Before we can critique others, we must first assess ourselves and recognize our flaws. You won't be aware of your own mistakes due to blind spots. When we let the Holy Spirit work in our lives, He will correct us and make known to us what has been kept secret. You can use your blind spots to heal once you become aware of them. Finding them improves your self-awareness and chances of growth.

You become more conscious of your advantages and strengths. Since anything that is not a strength gives us room to grow, I dislike using the word "weakness."

We all have blind spots that can obstruct our ability to heal because we are unable to see them or choose to ignore them. Let's examine the man at the Bethesda pool (John 5:1–18). This man had been lying by the pool for 38 years as an invalid, hoping to be the first person to enter the water once the angel disturbed it and heal his ailments. Jesus once left the temple and went down to the swimming area. He asked the man after noticing him in this situation. "Would you like to be made whole?" "Sir, I have no one to help me into the poos when the water is stirred," the man replied, not knowing who Jesus is or that The Healer is standing before him. *"While I am trying to get in, someone else goes down ahead of me."* WHAT!? Woe unto me! The reason I am not healed is that no one will help me. Did he not take notice that everyone at the pool was there for the same reason? This would be a blind spot for him. However, Jesus looks at him and says, *"Get up!" "Pick up your mat and walk."* As the man leaves, people begin to ask him who healed him on a Sabbath day, and he tells them, "The man did." HA!!! Being taken aback, he reverts to his stricken state. Later, Jesus is at the temple teaching, where he sees the man and goes over to him. Jesus says, *"See, you are well again." "Stop sinning, or something worse may happen to you."* Although the man's transgression is never brought up, we see Jesus heal him here a second time. The guy leaves this time, saying that Jesus had healed him.

Let's now examine how someone who is conscious of all their difficulties came to the conclusion that she was ultimately accountable for her healing and that no one could prevent her from experiencing it. Let's examine the woman who has a blood issue (Luke 8:43–48).

She was only known by the name of her problem, much like the man at the Bethesda pool. She was prohibited from being with others since, according to Jewish custom, everyone she touched would likewise be deemed ceremonially unclean. She had visited numerous doctors in an attempt to improve her condition, but none had been successful.Due to the problem, this woman had been cut off from everyone for twelve years. Could it be argued that this woman was in a dire situation? So when she learned about Jesus, she made the decision to be in charge of her own healing. Due to her proximity to Jesus in the throng, she made everyone she touched filthy, even Jesus. She nonetheless made her way through the crowd. and said, *"If I can only touch the hem of His garment, I will be healed."* As soon as she touches Jesus, the flow of blood ceases. In an instant, Jesus does what doctors have not been able to do. Her desperation was so powerful that it caused the very virtue of Jesus to leave His body, and He asked, *"Who touched me?"* Imagine the fear she must have felt because of the Jewish law.

Everyone was confused by Jesus' questioning because of the crowd and his denial that anyone touched Him. Jesus said, *"Someone touched me because power has left me."* The woman, seeing she could not go unnoticed, fell at the feet of Jesus, in the presence of all the people, and explained why she had touched Him and that she had been immediately healed. Jesus tells her, *"Daughter, your faith has made you whole." "Go in peace."* The woman with the blood issue accepted full responsibility for her own healing, but the man at the pool of Bethesda had permitted blind spots to obstruct his recovery.

Do you allow any blind spots to prevent you from accepting the gifts or requests God is making of you?

Things Change When You Take Responsibility & Action

My Self-Awareness Journey: WHO AM I?

Self-awareness happens through reflection on life experiences. Take the next seven days to step outside of your comfort zone to discover more about yourself. Instead of focusing on what others expect you to become, write about who you feel you are. Write about who you feel you are, not about what people expect you to become.

Write about your strengths and opportunities.

Day: _____   Date: _____

_____

_____

_____

_____

_____

_____

_____

_____

_____

_____

_____

_____

_____

_____

_____

Day: _____   Date: _____

_____

_____

_____

_____

_____

_____

_____

_____

_____

_____

_____

_____

_____

_____

_____

_____

Day: _____   Date: _____

_____

_____

_____

_____

_____

_____

_____

_____

_____

_____

_____

_____

_____

_____

_____

Day: _____   Date: _____

_____

_____

_____

_____

_____

_____

_____

_____

_____

_____

_____

_____

_____

_____

_____

_____

Day: _____   Date: _____

_____

_____

_____

_____

_____

_____

_____

_____

_____

_____

_____

_____

_____

_____

Day: _____   Date: _____

_____

_____

_____

_____

_____

_____

_____

_____

_____

_____

_____

_____

_____

_____

_____

_____

Day: _____   Date: _____

_____

_____

_____

_____

_____

_____

_____

_____

_____

_____

_____

_____

_____

_____

_____

Take It By FAITH

Read Luke 8:43-48. Take a moment to ponder on the woman.

1. Describe the woman and her condition.

2. In your own words, describe how she may have felt.

Read John 5:1-15. Take a moment to ponder on the man.

1. Describe the man and his condition.

2. In your own words, describe how he may have felt.

1. Describe the difference in the two individuals in the passages.

2. Which one of these people can you relate to the most?

3. What characteristics of the individual that relates to you the most do you demonstrate?

FAITH

is the key to

HEALING

1. What are your challenges?

2. Why are these challenges present?

CHAPTER SIX

WHOLE RELATIONSHIP:
CREATING HEALTHY BOUNDARIES

"The heart is hopelessly dark and deceitful, a puzzle that no one
can figure out. But I, God, search the heart and examine the mind.
I get to the heart of the human. I get to the root of things. I treat
Them as they really, not as they pretend to be."
JEREMIAH 17:9-10; MSG

Relationships should be a blessing rather than a burden. Setting limits is necessary if you find yourself in unsatisfactory relationships that cause more confusion than harmony. While those who have been healed allow God to bring them relationships to complement them, those who are broken look for relationships to complete them.

Setting boundaries doesn't necessarily include excluding someone from your life, even if it could be required occasionally. Our sense of self is safeguarded when we have personal boundaries in place, and it also helps us resist others' excessive demands. Respectable personal boundaries must be established in order to foster healthy interactions, reduce stress, and promote self-care and self-respect. Your physical, mental, and emotional health depend on it. When you don't establish limits, you run the risk of succumbing to someone else's chaos because they don't respect you.

According to Psychology Today, boundaries can be defined as the limits we set with other people, which indicate what we find acceptable and unacceptable in their behavior towards us. Boundaries can be physical and emotional.

Physical boundaries include your body, sense of personal space, and privacy. It outlines who can touch us, how they touch us, and how not allowing emotional boundaries protects your self-esteem and ability to separate your feelings.

We cannot control other people's behavior; therefore, we cannot always control being hurt. However, we can choose whether or not we will continue to allow individuals to commit the same patterns of behavior toward us that caused the pain. You have to take control of what you will or will not allow a person to do that crosses the boundary you have established with them.

Most times, we are afraid to enforce the boundaries we have set because we are afraid of offending the person who is disrespecting us, or we have not learned to set boundaries. Recognize that doing something you have never done before is difficult. Setting healthy boundaries requires practice and time. Start by setting smaller boundaries

Here are a few tips for setting healthy boundaries.

1. Know Yourself Better: Knowing yourself better will allow you to set appropriate boundaries.We occasionally enable others to breach boundaries with us because we don't recognize our own value and worth. Find out what matters and is appropriate for you. Without passing judgment, acknowledge your emotions. You can stay true to who you are by establishing limits. Pay attention to your emotions. What are you feeling? If you notice signs of discomfort, frustration, or resentment bubbling up inside you, don't bury them. Tune in to what is going on and ask yourself why you are feeling the way you are. Also, this may be a great opportunity to journal. It may reveal some underlying problems you have yet to address.

2. Make It Public—Communication Communication. Communication. Don't assume that others know the boundary you have set. Voicing your boundaries eliminates confusion. Most will respect the boundaries you have set if they are aware of them. You are responsible for communicating the boundary. Be direct but respectful.

NOTE: It is important to acknowledge what is acceptable as "safe" or "personal" space. People may have different beliefs and come from different cultures. So, whereas in one culture, touching may be considered a warm greeting, others may see it as offensive and disrespectful. What is important in situations like this is to clearly let others know when they are crossing a personal boundary. And remember, each person will have different personal boundaries. They are valid and need to be respected.

Write a letter to a person who hurt you, letting them know what boundaries they crossed in your relationship with them. Give specifics about the harm or offense that was committed against you. Describe how it affected you at the time and how it continues to hurt you.Describe what you would have done differently if you could. Finish by making a clear declaration of understanding and forgiveness, such as "I see now that what you did was the best you could at the time, and I forgive you."

Instead of writing for the benefit of the recipient, this type of letter is intended to aid in your own emotional processing. A decision to let go of animosity that is keeping you down might be made by writing a letter of forgiveness.

_____

_____

_____

_____

_____

_____

_____

_____

_____

_____

_____

_____

_____

_____

_____

_____

_____

BOUNDARIES AND BOUNDARY SETTING CHART

What is a Boundary:	
Write Down Personal Boundaries	**List Boundaries Being Crossed**
Who are Crossing These Boundaries?	**What Do You Need To Do To Set Healthy Boundaries?**

<u>REFLECTIONS</u>

<u>PRAYER</u>

CHAPTER SEVEN

WHOLE AGAIN:
INTENTIONAL HEALING

"Jesus is not a crutch for the weak. He is the source of new spiritual life!
When we're broken, He can make us new and whole."
PSALM 119:75

Going to the one who was fully capable of making me whole again was the key to my recovery. Without the Creator, it is impossible to become who you were intended to be. He tells us in Jeremiah 29:11–14a, *"For I know the plans I have for you, plans to prosper you and not to harm you, plans to give you hope and a future." Then you will call on me and come and pray to me, and I will listen to you. You will seek me and find me when you seek me with all your heart. "I will be found by you and will bring you back from captivity."* Often, we look to people and things to do what only God is able to do. We say things like, "If I find a man to marry, I will be complete; or if I have a baby, I will be complete; or if I have a good job, etc. Understand that no thing or person can ever fill the brokenness you have. What you are missing is internal, and to fill the void, you must do the necessary work.

I had spent almost twenty-five years broken in this world; then when I desired to be made whole, I found that I had to be broken again. But this time, by God. I can still remember the crushing. I was on the threshing floor. He was separating me from sin. He was disconnecting me from the hurt. He was disengaging me from the pain. He was taking away the guilt and shame. He was breaking me so He could heal me. Yes, it was painful, but it was for my good. I had to let go of the anger that I had towards those who caused the pain. I had to let go of the "should of," "could of," and "would of." I had to let go of the tight hold I had on them because it was seriously impacting me.

Without the threshing floor process, I would not have been able to grow into the person that God had in mind for me. The mental and emotional anguish brought on by the hurt I had suffered was like an infection in a deep wound. The cuts that were being made in this healing process penetrated my soul. I had to get rid of the pain that was ingrained in me and went well below the surface. It would be pointless to leave bad fruit and let the bitterness's root spread, cause trouble, and contaminate others. God was operating spiritually on my thoughts and emotions. He was relieving the suffering. I have to be able to forgive both myself and them. I have to assume accountability for my happiness and wellbeing.

Although the events of my past would not be altered, I could control how my future would be told. like you do! Put your focus on you, alter your way of thinking, and start your healing process if you wish to move past the problems in your past.

WHOLE VISION

Don't get stuck in places that should be temporary. By aligning yourself with God's plan, you give Him permission to guide you along the path He has already laid out for you.

Take control of your circumstances and learn to use them as stepping stones to move out of undesirable, non-prospering places. After assessing the problem, create an action plan to get through it.

You can develop your vision board and action plans on the pages that follow.

You may identify, focus, and maintain your attention on specific life goals with the aid of a vision board. Goal-setting is aided by vision boards, which are collages of images, encouraging words, and affirmations. They are visual aids made to assist you in picturing and acting on your future goals in order to make them come true.

You could obtain a better understanding of what you actually want by using a vision board to express your inner aims and wishes. It is meant to instill in you the courage to accept personal responsibility for the direction of your life.

Think about some attainable objectives you'd like to concentrate on before starting to make your vision board. These goals may also take into account your relationships, employment, finances, personal development, health, and other aspects.

To achieve your goals after making your vision board, you must create action plans. Be aware that there may be some challenges along the path, but do not allow this to stop you from making progress.

You may be unable to see clearly for a variety of reasons, including your relationship with the Father, your propensity to concentrate on what God is doing for others rather than what He is doing for you, unforgiveness, the inability to accept that you are worthy of what you desire, downplaying the authority of God's Word, and fear.

WRITE THE VISION

Make It Plain

Discover Your Strengths

Your Strengths

1. What are the strengths you've realized you can't live without? Why?

2. How are your strengths being used in your present life?

3. What qualities are you most proud of? Why?

4. With what combination of strengths have you successfully completed something?

(Opportunities) Unexplored Strengths

1. What unexplored strengths would you like to develop?

2. What might you need to change to make it happen?

3. What goal could you set that would encourage you to use them more?

Achieving Your Goals

Recognize your strengths and how they might help you overcome challenges to reach your goals.

Goal :

Strengthening your goal

What strengths would support your goal?

How would it support your goal?

What actions will lead you towards your goal?

Challenging your goal

What weaknesses can impact your goal?

How would it affect your goal?

What strengths will support you?

Setting Your Goals

ACTION PLAN

30 DAYS

ACTION PLAN

60 DAYS

ACTION PLAN

90 DAYS

ACTION PLAN

Long Term Goal(s):	Strategy #1			
	Strategy #2			
	Strategy #3			
	Strategy #4			
Additional Strategies:				
Annual Retreat:				
Annual Vision Board Workshop:				

Long Term Goal(s):	Strategy #1			
	Strategy #2			
	Strategy #3			
	Strategy #4			
Additional Strategies:				
Annual Retreat:				
Annual Vision Board Workshop				

Long Term Goal(s):	Strategy #1			
	Strategy #2			
	Strategy #3			
	Strategy #4			
Additional Strategies:				
Annual Retreat:				
Annual Vision Board Workshop				

JOURNAL ENTRY

Journal writing is an effective tool for healing. It's critical to be honest about your wounds. By jotting down your ideas and feelings, journaling can aid in your personal growth.

Tips:

1. Make a list of your hurts; next to each one, write down anything you believe is preventing you from moving past it, as well as what you need to do to move ahead.
2. Write in your journal about your emotional, mental, and spiritual state.
3. Without considering what you are writing, write for 5 to 10 minutes.
4. Start a dialogue with your inner child. Write with your less dominant hand what your inner child would like to express. Then answer with your dominant hand to see what emerges.
5. Write down your successes and how they make you feel.
6. Use additional techniques that motivate you to journal (take a walk, listen to inspirational music, then journal your thoughts).

_____

_____

_____

_____

_____

_____

_____

_____

_____

_____

_____

_____

_____

_____

_____

_____

_____

_____

_____

_____

_____

_____

_____

_____

_____

_____

_____

_____

_____

_____

_____

_____

_____

_____

_____

_____

_____

_____

_____

_____

_____

_____

_____

_____

_____

_____

_____

_____

_____

_____

_____

_____

_____

_____

_____

_____

_____

_____

_____

_____

_____

_____

_____

_____

_____

_____

_____

_____

_____

_____

_____

_____

_____

_____

_____

_____

_____

_____

_____

_____

_____

_____

_____

_____

_____

_____

_____

_____

_____

_____

_____

_____

_____

_____

_____

_____

_____

_____

_____

_____

_____

_____

_____

_____

_____

_____

_____

_____

_____

_____

_____

_____

_____

_____

_____

_____

_____

_____

_____

_____

_____

_____

_____

_____

_____

_____

_____

_____

_____

_____

_____

_____

_____

_____

_____

_____

_____

_____

_____

_____

_____

_____

www.ingramcontent.com/pod-product-compliance
Lightning Source LLC
Chambersburg PA
CBHW050658110426
42739CB00035B/3450